United States Government Accountability Office

GAO

Report to the Subcommittee on Commerce, Justice, Science, and Related Agencies, Committee on Appropriations, House of Representatives

January 2012

DEPARTMENT OF JUSTICE

Working Capital Fund Adheres to Some Key Operating Principles but Could Better Measure Performance and Communicate with Customers

GAO

Accountability * Integrity * Reliability

GAO
Accountability * Integrity * Reliability

Highlights

Highlights of GAO-12-289, a report to the Subcommittee on Commerce, Justice, Science, and Related Agencies, Committee on Appropriations, House of Representatives

January 2012

DEPARTMENT OF JUSTICE

Working Capital Fund Adheres to Some Key Operating Principles but Could Better Measure Performance and Communicate with Customers

Why GAO Did This Study

The Department of Justice's (Justice) working capital fund is intended to provide increased efficiencies in how the department funds and offers shared services—such as payroll, telecommunications, financial services, mail, and publications—valued at over $1 billion annually. Ensuring that the working capital fund is managed as efficiently as possible could allow Justice to use saved resources for other departmental priorities. GAO was asked to determine how Justice (1) manages its working capital fund to promote compliance with applicable fiscal laws and key operating principles, (2) communicates shared services rates with customers, (3) measures performance to evaluate whether fund activities are contributing to agency goals, and (4) ensures that its excess unobligated balances are used in accordance with legal authorities and managed so that Justice can make well-informed funding decisions. GAO reviewed statutory authorities, analyzed Justice policies, interviewed budget and finance officials, and conducted focus groups with some shared services customers.

What GAO Recommends

GAO is making three recommendations to improve the management of the working capital fund, including providing opportunities for two-way substantive communications with customers and developing performance measures for the fund. Justice generally agreed with our findings and recommendations and noted that it will continue to explore ways to address the issues we identified.

View GAO-12-289. For more information, contact Denise M. Fantone at (202) 512-6806 or fantoned@gao.gov.

What GAO Found

The Justice Management Division (JMD), the component responsible for managing the working capital fund, effectively tracks fund functions to ensure adherence to applicable fiscal laws and sound management practices. For example, JMD has well-established policies and procedures for tracking and monitoring the four working capital fund functions so that the fund adheres to authorized purposes. Further, JMD structures its reimbursable agreements with customers to facilitate adherence to the Economy Act—the statutory authority underlying most of JMD's customer orders. JMD also clearly delineates roles and responsibilities, which allows customers to know who to contact with questions and clearly assigns responsibility for obligating and expending funds. Justice also ensures the fund's self-sufficiency by recovering total costs for the provided services. These actions are consistent with two of the four key operating principles for working capital funds.

Customers noted positive benefits from Justice's shared services but seek more information on rate structures and want assurances that fund costs are equitably distributed. For example, customers said they valued the breadth of services offered as well as the experience of fund staff but wanted to better understand the basis for shared services rates and more opportunities to discuss billing concerns and service changes with JMD. Officials expressed surprise at these concerns. They noted that informal information sharing on rates and rate structures happens regularly, but explained that each staff director has his/her own way of communicating with customers and acknowledged that some may be better at providing customer support than others.

JMD does not systematically measure important aspects of shared service provision and working capital fund management. For example, JMD tracks workload measures such as the number of transactions processed, but does not assess customer satisfaction with shared services. It also does not have measures to assess how effectively it manages the fund, such as whether managers are responsive to concerns about shared service rates or billing issues—areas with which customers have expressed concern. Absent a formal mechanism for customers to provide timely and regular feedback, JMD cannot sufficiently assess whether customer needs are met or have changed. JMD also has not assessed its shared services rates to know whether they provide a good value to customers. If available, specific working capital fund-level performance information would allow JMD to regularly compare actual performance with planned or expected performance. Further, a corresponding management review process could help JMD achieve the efficiencies that working capital funds were designed to produce, potentially freeing up resources that could be realigned for other departmental initiatives. Lastly, performance measures aligned with strategic goals can be used to evaluate whether and how working capital fund activities contribute to departmentwide goals and crosscutting initiatives.

Justice has processes to ensure that excess unobligated balances are used in accordance with legal authorities. It also has an established process to make well-informed decisions on how to spend available funds. However, JMD budget officials told us that these balances were unavailable for departmentwide priorities in recent years because they have been used to meet rescissions.

_____ **United States Government Accountability Office**

Contents

Figures

Abbreviations

AAG/A	Assistant Attorney General for Administration
AFF	Assets Forfeiture Fund
CAB	Customer Advisory Board
DHS	Department of Homeland Security
FMIS	Financial Management Information System
FTE	full-time equivalent
JMD	Justice Management Division
OBD	Offices, Boards, and Divisions
OMB	Office of Management and Budget
UBT	Unobligated Balance Transfers

United States Government Accountability Office
Washington, DC 20548

January 20, 2012

The Honorable Frank R. Wolf
Chairman
The Honorable Chaka Fattah
Ranking Member
Subcommittee on Commerce, Justice, Science, and Related Agencies
Committee on Appropriations
House of Representatives

One way federal agencies can increase their efficiency and reduce costs is to share services. The Department of Justice's (Justice) working capital fund is intended, in part, to provide increased efficiencies and flexibilities in the funding and provision of centralized, administrative shared services.[1] These services include, among other things, telecommunications, financial services, mail, publications, and payroll valued at over $1 billion annually. Working capital funds and other types of intragovernmental revolving funds enable agencies to operate more efficiently by consolidating and providing services used by multiple organizations within an agency. Ensuring that the working capital fund is managed as efficiently as possible could allow Justice to use saved resources for other departmental priorities.

Intragovernmental revolving funds include working capital, franchise, and other similar types of funds. They are self-supporting and used to conduct businesslike activities within and between federal agencies. In general, intragovernmental revolving funds allow agencies to benefit from economies of scale or take advantage of specialized expertise that the agency may not have. A market-like atmosphere is intended to create incentives for customers and fund managers to exercise cost control and economic restraint.

This report is the third in a series in response to the subcommittee's request to review the management of intragovernmental revolving funds, the shared services they support, and unobligated carryover balances in those funds. It builds on our work at the National Institute of Standards

---

[1] Justice refers to its subagencies, such as the Federal Bureau of Investigation and the Drug Enforcement Administration, as components.

and Technology,[2] the Department of Commerce, and the U.S. Census Bureau.[3] For this report, we were asked to determine (1) how Justice manages its working capital fund to promote compliance with applicable fiscal laws and key operating principles, (2) the effectiveness of Justice's communications with working capital fund customers and its efforts to ensure that its shared services rates are equitably distributed, (3) the effectiveness of Justice's performance measures in evaluating whether working capital fund activities are contributing to the achievement of agency goals, and (4) how Justice ensures that its excess unobligated balances in the working capital fund and the Assets Forfeiture Fund (AFF) are used in accordance with legal authorities and managed in a way that allow Justice to make well-informed agencywide funding decisions.[4]

For the first objective, we reviewed relevant legislation and statutory authorities that govern Justice's working capital fund, as well as Justice's documented policies and procedures for managing, tracking, and monitoring funds deposited into the fund. To determine to what extent Justice adhered to sound management principles, we referred to guidance on internal controls and cost accounting as well as relevant Justice Inspector General reports.[5] Additionally, we used recently developed and compiled criteria on key operating principles for working capital funds. To identify these principles, we reviewed governmentwide guidance on business operating principles, internal controls, managerial

---

[2] GAO, *Intragovernmental Revolving Funds: NIST's Interagency Agreements and Workload Require Management Attention*, GAO-11-41 (Washington, D.C.: Oct. 20, 2010).

[3] GAO, *Intragovernmental Revolving Funds: Commerce Departmental and Census Working Capital Funds Should Better Reflect Key Operating Principles*, GAO-12-56 (Washington, D.C.: Nov. 18, 2011).

[4] Justice's AFF is a nationwide law enforcement program. The principal mission of AFF is to disrupt and dismantle criminal organizations by depriving them of the use of the economic proceeds of their crimes and of assets used to facilitate their crimes. Federal employees, contract personnel, and foreign, state, and local law enforcement officials work cooperatively in investigating and prosecuting cases involving asset seizure and forfeiture to support the program's mission.

[5] GAO, *Standards for Internal Control in the Federal Government*, GAO/AIMD-00-21.3.1 (Washington, D.C.: November 1999); Federal Accounting Standards Advisory Board, *Statement of Federal Financial Accounting Standards No. 4: Managerial Cost Accounting Standards and Concepts and Standards for the Federal Government* (Washington, D.C.: July 31, 1995); and Department of Justice Inspector General, *Top Management and Performance Challenges in the Department of Justice – 2010* (Washington, D.C.: Nov. 9, 2010).

cost accounting, and performance management. Our prior work on user fees, franchise funds, performance management, and customer service also informed the development of these principles. We also met with staff from the Office of Management and Budget (OMB) to obtain their views, and they found the principles to be reasonable.[6]

For the second objective, we reviewed Justice's policies and procedures for setting and reviewing rates and collecting charges and its process for communicating with its customers. Additionally, we referred to our prior work on federal user fees, as appropriate.[7] We examined the rate-setting process for services provided through the working capital fund; however, we did not independently verify whether the process resulted in equitable distribution of costs among customers or in the recovery of total costs.

For the third objective, we reviewed the working capital fund's customer feedback mechanisms as well as performance and workload evaluation tools. Additionally, we reviewed the fund's performance measures and the data it collects to assess its performance.

For the fourth objective, we reviewed Justice's legal authorities as well as the policies and procedures governing the use of excess unobligated balances within its working capital fund and AFF. We also reviewed congressional notifications and budget documents to understand how these balances have been used.

For all objectives, we interviewed senior management, budget, and finance staff from the Justice Management Division (JMD), the Justice component that manages the working capital fund. Additionally, we met with representatives of the working capital fund's Customer Advisory Board (CAB) as well as staff from the finance divisions of selected working capital fund customers. Specifically, Justice provided access to six of the eight Justice components represented on the CAB. We conducted focus groups with five of these board members and met separately with a sixth member who was unable to attend the focus group. Additionally, we conducted separate focus groups with representatives from 13 customer components—about half of all

---

[6] GAO-12-56.

[7] GAO, *Federal User Fees: A Design Guide*, GAO-08-386SP (Washington, D.C.: May 29, 2008).

customers not on the advisory board. To develop and analyze themes emerging from our focus groups and interviews, we conducted a content analysis of participants' discussions and responses to our questions.

We conducted this performance audit from January 2011 to January 2012 in accordance with generally accepted government auditing standards. Those standards require that we plan and perform the audit to obtain sufficient, appropriate evidence to provide a reasonable basis for our findings and conclusions based on our audit objectives. We believe that the evidence obtained provides a reasonable basis for our findings and conclusions based on our audit objectives.

Background

Justice's Working Capital Fund Serves Four Functions

JMD has overall responsibility for managing the working capital fund and AFF. Justice's working capital fund was created by Congress on January 2, 1975. The fund is authorized to maintain moneys from four distinct sources, or functions (see table 1). The first and primary function of the fund is to finance, on a reimbursable basis, administrative shared services provided by JMD to other components of the department and other federal agencies. The second function of the working capital fund is to collect up to 3 percent of funds collected pursuant to civil debt collection litigation activities into the fund. A third function of the working capital fund is to collect up to 4 percent of earnings from its shared services provision. Finally, the working capital fund's fourth function is to capture expired departmental unobligated balances into the working capital fund's Unobligated Balance Transfers (UBT) account. Because the working capital fund is a no-year account, all amounts earned or collected by the fund are available without fiscal year limitation to be used for specific authorized purposes. For example, amounts from three of the four working capital fund functions may be used for capital equipment investments and financial system improvements.

Table 1: Justice's Working Capital Fund Functions

Authorized functions	Source of funds	How these funds can be spent
Provision of shared services FY 2010 revenue: $1.2 billion	Costs for goods and services are collected from customers. Justice charges rates that cover the total expenses, including accrued annual leave and overhead costs.	• Continue working capital fund operations • Future capital and equipment investments
Debt collection improvement FY 2010 revenue: $102 million	Justice is authorized to credit up to 3 percent of amounts pursuant to civil debt collection litigation activities.	Funds must be used in the following order: • Paying the costs of processing and tracking civil and criminal debt collection litigation • Paying financial systems and debt collection-related personnel, administrative, and litigation expenses
Four percent retention FY 2010 surplus: $38 million	Justice is authorized to retain up to 4 percent of the total shared services earnings each fiscal year.	Upon notification to the Senate and House Committees on Appropriations, these funds can be used for the following: • Acquiring capital equipment • Improving and implementing Justice's financial management and personnel systems
Unobligated Balance Transfers FY 2010 deposits: $75 million	Justice is authorized to transfer expired unobligated balances into the working capital fund from other Justice accounts.	Upon notification to the Senate and House Committees on Appropriations, these funds can be used for the following: • Financing Justice-wide capital equipment acquisition • Developing and implementing law enforcement or litigation-related automated data processing systems • Improving and implementing the department's financial management and payroll/personnel systems

Source: GAO analysis based on Justice documents.

The largest portion of the working capital fund comes from charges for centralized administrative and infrastructure support services and functions collected on a reimbursable basis from Justice components. The shared services provided by the working capital fund are generally commercial functions, such as data processing, publications, building services, financial operations, employee data, telecommunications, property management, and space management (see working capital fund services and support in fig. 1).

While most Justice components use the working capital fund to obtain administrative shared services, there is no statutory requirement that they do so. For fiscal year 2010, Justice's largest customers were the U.S. Attorney's Office, JMD, the Bureau of Prisons, the Federal Bureau of Investigation, and the Drug Enforcement Administration (see customers in fig. 1). Some services are also available to other federal agencies. For example, the Department of Homeland Security (DHS) was the largest non-Justice customer of the working capital fund. The working capital fund received $38 million from DHS in fiscal year 2010 for information technology services. However, JMD officials told us that DHS is exiting the working capital fund and its remaining agreements with the fund are expected to be completed by fiscal year 2013.

Figure 1: Working Capital Fund Services and Customers for Fiscal Year 2010

Directions:
Mouseover the highlighted "Other services" and "All other customers" wedges of the two pie charts below for expanded program listings.

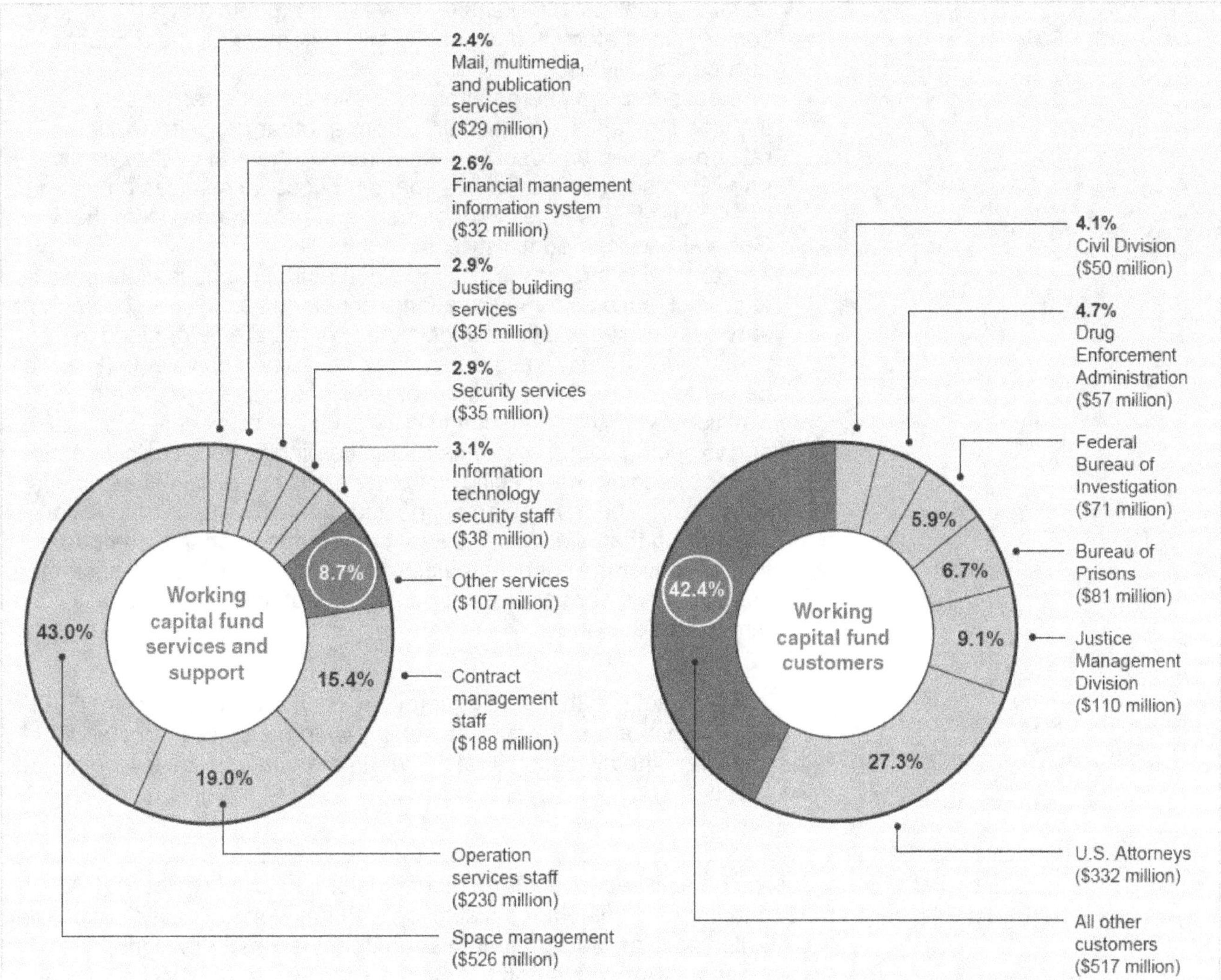

2.4%
Mail, multimedia, and publication services
($29 million)

2.6%
Financial management information system
($32 million)

2.9%
Justice building services
($35 million)

2.9%
Security services
($35 million)

3.1%
Information technology security staff
($38 million)

8.7%

Other services
($107 million)

43.0%

Working capital fund services and support

15.4%

Contract management staff
($188 million)

19.0%

Operation services staff
($230 million)

Space management
($526 million)

4.1%
Civil Division
($50 million)

4.7%
Drug Enforcement Administration
($57 million)

Federal Bureau of Investigation
($71 million)

5.9%

Bureau of Prisons
($81 million)

6.7%

Justice Management Division
($110 million)

9.1%

42.4%

Working capital fund customers

27.3%

U.S. Attorneys
($332 million)

All other customers
($517 million)

Source: GAO analysis of Department of Justice information.

Print instructions | For a printable text version of this graphic, go to appendix I.

To set and review rates for working capital fund services, JMD develops, in the context of Justice's budget formulation process, an annual 2-year operating plan. As a part of developing the operating plans, JMD sets the rates for its services using one of three strategies.

- The "dollar-per-widget" strategy aligns rates with the cost of the service provided. JMD creates an internal cost schedule of these services that lists, for example, how much a photocopy or scan job costs. This strategy is designed to bill customers for the amount of service actually used.
- The pass-through charge strategy is used to set rates for services that the working capital fund acquires from another provider. Customer rates are based on costs as determined by the non-Justice service providers, such as the flexible spending account services provided by the Office of Personnel Management and rent charges from the General Services Administration.
- The allocation strategy is applied when actual usage is more difficult to predict, such as for information technology security, e-government services, and acquisition support. Allocations are determined in various ways, such as a percentage of full-time equivalents (FTE), a percentage of budget authority, or a weighted average of both. Additionally, JMD staff factor in data such as recent cost information and expected use of a service for the coming year. To calculate the estimated cost for a specific customer, JMD reviews the customer's actual use in prior years and expected use for the upcoming fiscal year. From that, JMD calculates a percentage to charge customers that will cover the cost of providing that level of service. All customers using a service are charged a percentage of total estimated costs throughout the year.

JMD officials told us that they generally apply the dollar-per-widget and pass-through charge strategies in setting shared services rates and that they only use the allocation strategy when the other strategies would not work well.

Working Capital Fund Customer Advisory Board

Justice established its eight-member Customer Advisory Board (CAB) in 1994 to improve customer satisfaction with the working capital fund. The CAB also advises JMD on fund management issues. The eight components represented on the CAB are the Bureau of Alcohol, Tobacco, Firearms and Explosives; Bureau of Prisons; Drug Enforcement Administration; Federal Bureau of Investigation; General Legal Activities; U.S. Attorneys; U.S. Marshals Service; and Office of Inspector General.

JMD elected these eight components to be members of the CAB because they were the working capital fund's largest customers. JMD convenes an annual meeting with CAB members at the beginning of each fiscal year to present the updated operating plan and selected purchases for the year.

Working Capital Fund Key Operating Principles

We have previously identified the following four key operating principles to guide the management of working capital funds.[8] For further information about the four key principles and their underlying components, see figure 2.

- **Clearly delineate roles and responsibilities**: Appropriate delineation of roles and responsibilities promotes a clear understanding of who will be held accountable for specific tasks or duties, such as authorizing and reviewing transactions, implementing controls over working capital fund management, and helping ensure that related responsibilities are coordinated. In addition, this reduces the risk of mismanaged funds and tasks or functions "falling through the cracks." Moreover, it helps customers know who to contact if they have questions.
- **Ensure self-sufficiency by recovering the agency's actual costs**: Transparent and equitable pricing methodologies allow agencies to ensure that rates charged recover the agencies' actual costs and reflect customers' service usage. If customers understand how rates are determined or changed—including the assumptions used—customers can better anticipate potential changes to those assumptions, identify their effect on costs, and incorporate that information into budget plans. A management review process can help to ensure that the methodology is applied consistently over time and provides a forum to inform customers of decisions and discuss as needed.
- **Measure performance**: Performance goals and measures are important management tools applicable to all operations of an agency, including the program, project, or activity levels. Performance measures and goals could include targets that assess fund managers' responsiveness to customer inquiries, the consistency in the application of the funds' rate-setting methodology, and the billing error rates. Performance measures that are aligned with strategic goals can be used to evaluate whether and, if so, how working capital fund

---

[8] GAO-12-56.

activities are contributing to the achievement of agency goals. A management review process comparing expected to actual performance allows agencies to review progress toward goals and potentially identify ways to improve performance.

- **Build in flexibility to obtain customer input and meet customer needs**: Opportunities for customers to provide input about working capital fund services or voice concerns about needs in a timely manner enable agencies to regularly assess whether customer needs are being met or have changed. This also enables agencies to prioritize customer demands and use resources most effectively, enabling them to adjust working capital fund capacity up or down as business rises or falls.

By incorporating these principles in written guidance, agencies promote consistent application of management processes and provide a baseline for agency officials to assess and improve management processes. Moreover, agencies can use guidance as a training tool for new staff and as an information tool for customers, program managers, stakeholders, and reviewers.

Interactive graphic Figure 2: Working Capital Fund Key Operating Principles

 Directions:

Mouseover **Description** buttons for definitions of key principles and **Example** buttons to see examples of evidence that support key principles.

Key principle	Components of principle	
Clearly delineate roles and responsibilities Description	Segregate duties to reduce error or fraud	Example
	Define key areas of authority and responsibility	Example
	Establish management review and approval process at the functional or activity level that ensures appropriate tracking and use of funds	Example
Ensure self-sufficiency by recovering the agency's actual costs Description	Establish transparent and equitable pricing methodology	Example
	Set rates to cover agency's actual costs of providing service	Example
	Establish management review process for rate setting	Example
Measure performance Description	Establish performance measures and goals	Example
	Align performance measures with strategic goals	Example
	Establish management review of working capital fund performance	Example
Build in flexibility to obtain customer input and meet customer needs Description	Communicate with customers regularly and in a timely manner	Example
	Develop process to assess resources needed to meet changes in customer demand	Example
	Establish process to prioritize requests for services	Example

Source: GAO analysis.

 **Print instructions** | To print text version of this graphic, go to appendix II.

GAO-12-289 Working Capital Fund

JMD Effectively Tracks Working Capital Fund Moneys in Accordance with Fiscal Law and Aspects of Key Operating Principles

JMD Effectively Tracks Working Capital Fund Functions to Ensure Adherence to Authorized Purposes and Applicable Fiscal Laws

JMD has well-established policies and procedures for tracking and monitoring each of the four working capital fund functions to adhere to authorized purposes. JMD uses its financial management system, the Financial Management Information System (FMIS), to track moneys by project codes to distinguish among the different working capital fund functions. Additionally, Justice's written policies direct the head of each component to maintain a financial accounting system with internal controls in place to ensure effective management and disbursement of federal funds. FMIS also supports the departmentwide fund control system; it is designed to restrict both obligations and expenditures from each appropriation or fund account to the amount available for obligation or expenditure.

Since 1984, all working capital fund moneys are identified and tracked using reimbursement code numbers so that JMD can identify the source of all funds and monitor obligations established against the working capital fund's partitioned subaccounts related to each of the fund's four functions. Balances associated with each function are tracked in separate partitions in the working capital fund and remain available until expended. This ensures that the funds associated with the four working capital fund functions are tracked and managed to ensure that they are used in accordance with its authorities.[9]

---

[9] According to JMD officials, retained earnings have been primarily used for the consolidated financial management and travel systems. Civil debt funds have been used in the order authorized and primarily for processing and tracking civil and criminal debt-collection litigation. JMD adheres to notification requirements for the 4 percent retention and the unobligated balance transfer functions.

JMD structures its reimbursable agreements with customers in a way that facilitates adherence to the Economy Act—the statutory authority underlying most of the shared services orders received from customers.[10] For example, Justice aligns its agreements to coincide with a single fiscal year and has policies against accepting advanced funds from federal customers (instead, Justice generally receives reimbursements after providing shared services). This helps Justice and its customers comply with the Economy Act's deobligation requirements and mitigates the risk of using appropriated funds when they are not legally available.

Justice's policies also require that JMD establish an accurate and reliable tracking system to monitor, on an ongoing and consistent basis, obligations established against reimbursable agreements for billing purposes. Justice has issued guidance on how JMD should manage payments to the working capital fund so that those amounts are accurately recorded and controlled, and ensure that anticipated and actual reimbursements for goods or services provided are properly recorded. Further, Justice's policies govern how JMD controls and monitors shared services funds and describe the responsibilities of both the provider and customer. For example, these policies task JMD, in the role of the service provider, with the responsibility of monitoring reimbursements anticipated, earned, billed, unbilled, and collected, in relation to the agreed-upon agreement amount. Customers are responsible for monitoring the status of reimbursable services performed but not yet billed to ensure that obligations recorded are sufficient to pay for the shared services they receive. In responding to a draft of this report, Justice officials also noted that the service providers convey the status of the reimbursable agreements to the customers quarterly.

JMD Adheres to Aspects of Two Key Operating Principles to Manage the Working Capital Fund

To clearly delineate roles and responsibilities, JMD clearly defines key areas of authority, responsibilities, and roles within the working capital fund. This allows customers to know who to contact if they have questions. Justice describes this information in a departmentwide funds control order. These delineated roles and responsibilities are posted on the working capital fund web page and are available to both internal and external customers as well as the general public. Key working capital fund

---

[10] 31 U.S.C. § 1535.

duties and responsibilities are spread among multiple individuals and offices. For example:

- The Assistant Attorney General for Administration (AAG/A) is the fund's general manager and approves all final decisions and major initiatives affecting customers.
- The Deputy Assistant Attorney General, Controller (DAAG-Controller), is the financial manager of the working capital fund and is responsible for overseeing budgets.
- Staff directors ensure service delivery to customers, develop operating plans and rate structure, produce customer billings, and are responsible for day-to-day fund management.
- Budget staff review and monitor all working capital fund budgets and make recommendations about the funding initiatives and rate changes requested by staff directors.

JMD has also clearly defined the responsibilities for the administrative control of working capital funds. JMD has established policies and guidance regarding roles and responsibilities for obligating and expending funds. Specifically, financial management policies state that the AAG/A is the department's Chief Financial Officer with responsibilities that include direction and oversight of JMD's financial procedures, practices, operations, systems, and internal controls. In addition, the component heads are responsible for accurate, timely, and complete financial data. These written roles and responsibilities specify how key duties are spread among multiple individuals and can help customers understand who does what. The information is also sufficiently detailed to be useful for internal JMD purposes, such as training and succession planning.

To ensure self-sufficiency by recovering the agency's actual costs, another key working capital fund operating principle, JMD generally charges rates that cover the total cost of providing shared services.[11] It bases customer charges on both estimated direct and indirect costs. JMD estimates direct costs based on historical data trends and the actual costs of providing that service. JMD uses an overhead allocation methodology to determine the administrative costs of providing shared services, which

---

[11] JMD officials said that cross subsidization of accounts allows the working capital fund to recover the total costs of providing shared services at the fund level.

are then spread to each shared services account and collected from customers as part of the overall rate structure.

As part of its annual 2-year operating plan process, JMD ensures that rates remain aligned with total costs of operations. JMD staff review the rates by conducting a line-by-line review of each shared services account to determine how costs will change for the coming year. JMD factors forecasted revenue and rate changes based on historical and market data into its shared services rates.

JMD's strategy is to recover total cost at the fund level. Although JMD's goal is for each shared services account to break even, JMD officials said that some lines of business generate income while others operate at a loss. For example, officials told us that certain services, such as data center services, have recovered more than their actual costs while others, such as the audiovisual and photography services, do not always fully recover costs. Recovering costs at the fund level results in some amount of cross subsidization between various services, which can help ensure that the fund remains solvent.

Customers Noted Positive Benefits of Shared Services but Need More Information on Rates, Costs, and Billing, and More Opportunities for Substantive, Two-way Communication

Customers Noted Some Positive Benefits of the Working Capital Fund's Shared Services Provision

During our focus groups and interviews, customers said that they find the working capital fund's shared services to be valuable.[12] For example, customers cited the breadth of services offered as well as the experience and knowledge of shared services staff as key strengths of the fund. Further, two customers said that they appreciated the convenience and ease of having these services provided in-house. However, as we will discuss below, CAB members we spoke with were concerned about their limited advisory role, and customers in our focus groups were concerned about how JMD communicates with customers about working capital fund rates and billing information. These customers wanted more opportunities for substantive, two-way communication with the working capital fund staff directors. JMD officials explained that each working capital fund staff director has his or her own way of communicating and interacting with customers and acknowledged that some may be better at providing customer support than others.

---

[12] We conducted three focus groups with working capital fund customers. Specifically, we met with six of the eight CAB members and 13 other working capital fund customers from Justice. In total, we met with 19 customers who represented 15 Justice components.

Customers Would Like More Information on Rate Structures and Assurance That Rates Are Equitably Distributed

Customers had different perspectives on whether shared services rates were fair. Two customers told us that they believe the working capital fund negotiates the best rates on their behalf, but one of these customers pointed out that his component lacked information that would ensure the staff of this. Other customers said that without information proving otherwise, they assume that they pay more than what it costs for JMD to provide the service. Customers also noted that they would like more transparency related to the earnings that JMD generates from rates set using the allocation strategy and how it affects actual shared services charges. For example, one customer noted that when determining the rates for e-mail services—whose rates are determined using the allocation strategy—basing rates on total FTE counts is less accurate than basing the rate on the actual number of staff using the service. Generally, customers indicated that they would have a greater sense of comfort with shared services rates if they better understood what they were based on.

JMD officials expressed surprise at these concerns. They said that information sharing on rates and rate structures happens regularly on an informal basis and in forums, such as monthly budget officer meetings, and that information about the shared services rates is available in various places depending on the service. For example, they said that some shared services rate information is available on Justice's intranet pages and that the cover memos accompanying the reimbursable agreements for certain services contain substantial amounts of information about how the rates are set each year. Further, with respect to e-mail rates, they said that they base the charges on the number of active e-mail accounts at the end of the prior fiscal year and that they adopted this allocation strategy in response to customer feedback. Specifically, officials said that in the past, JMD billed e-mail charges based on monthly counts of active e-mail accounts but that CAB members found the variability in billings too difficult to plan for and instead preferred paying a set monthly charge. JMD officials told us that as a result, the working capital fund now charge for e-mail services based on the active number of e-mail accounts at the end of the prior fiscal year, and that they adjust their counts annually.

Currently, JMD officials directly communicate the basis for shared services rates only with CAB members at the annual meeting and do not have a formalized mechanism to do so with customers not on the board. In response to a question about how non-CAB customers would receive rate information, JMD officials explained that this information is included in the operating plan. Further, they said that there is a board member responsible for sharing relevant portions of the operating plan with all of the department's direct reports and other customers. However, JMD officials did not know whether this process is working as intended. It is also unclear whether the CAB member with the responsibility for sharing information with non-CAB members has the necessary knowledge of rate structures and changes as they apply to other components. Transparent and equitable pricing methodologies allow agencies to ensure that rates charged recover agencies' actual costs and reflect customers' service usage. If customers understand how rates are determined, they can better anticipate changes to assumptions, identify their effect on costs, and incorporate this information into their budget planning.

Most Customers Want More Opportunities for Substantive, Two-way Communication with JMD

Absent regular opportunities for a substantive two-way exchange of information, miscommunications such as those described above are unlikely to be resolved. Most customers we spoke with—both CAB members and nonmembers—said that they want more opportunities for a substantive exchange of information with JMD. For example, the majority of CAB members we met with said that because they historically have not received information about changes to shared services rates prior to the annual meeting and feel unprepared to have a substantive discussion about the operating plan and provide input on other management issues. JMD officials responded to this by saying that the annual meeting is not intended to be the only or primary vehicle for engaging their customers. Rather, they view the CAB meeting as the first step in the communications process and see the annual board meeting as an executive-level overview of fund issues for the coming year. They also said that they have always provided opportunities for and encouraged feedback and questions about the materials after the meeting, and that CAB members sometimes provide written and oral responses.

JMD officials said that although staff directors occasionally provide some component-specific rate information upon request prior to the annual meeting, they have historically not provided advance copies of the operating plan, proposed rates, or both for three reasons. First, JMD officials explained that it is difficult to provide that information early because of the timing of when the plan is finalized and when the CAB meetings must occur. JMD officials said that they begin the operating plan process late in the fiscal year to ensure that updated data are available to adjust rates for the coming year. At the same time, the meeting needs to occur early in the fiscal year so that CAB members can approve the operating plan, which includes updated shared services rates that will be used to renew reimbursable agreements with customers. Second, officials were concerned about sharing a draft plan that had not been finalized. Lastly, JMD officials were concerned that if they provided the information in advance, CAB members would focus too exclusively on component-specific details and limit the group's ability to engage in a high-level discussion about the fund. This year, in response to discussions about preliminary observations from focus groups conducted as part of our review, JMD provided CAB members with the operating plan about a week before the annual meeting. A JMD official said that one member acknowledged the usefulness of receiving materials in advance. Further, the JMD official noted that there were fewer questions about the operating plan than in past years, but could not directly attribute this to having sent the operating plan out ahead of time.

CAB members also want more substantive two-way communications during the board meetings. Board members told us that the structure of the annual CAB meeting does not allow for this type of exchange. They said that because most of the meeting consists of briefings by JMD, there is limited opportunity for members to ask questions or provide input on fund operations. JMD officials told us that one way they solicit the opinions of CAB members is by asking them to vote on whether certain large investments should be made in the coming year, though they also acknowledged that CAB members have not voted on many issues in recent years. CAB members, however, do not view voting as a means for substantive input since the votes are on very specific issues that do not relate to how the working capital fund is managed.

JMD has no formal venue to communicate with non-CAB customers; however, JMD officials told us that customers have a variety of avenues to learn more about the shared services they purchase. For example, JMD staff said that they meet monthly with the executive officers and budget officers, that they attach cover memos to the reimbursable agreements that contain information about the rates and services, and that general information about the shared services and working capital fund is available on Justice's intranet site. Nevertheless, customers want more opportunities to learn about upcoming service enhancements or changes. JMD officials told us that they have taken steps, such as those mentioned above, to improve communications with customers and that they remain committed to doing so. Although communication is clearly a shared responsibility between the customer and the shared services provider, effectively communicating with customers involves sharing relevant analysis and information as well as providing opportunities for customer input. Agencies that do not communicate effectively with stakeholders miss opportunities for meaningful feedback that could affect the outcome of changes in both rates and program implementation.

JMD Does Not Always Provide Customers with Timely, Clear Billing Information

Customer experiences with getting clear, timely, well-explained bills for working capital fund services are mixed. On the one hand, a customer noted that the library service provides clear, detailed, and complete billing information that is easily accessible online. The customer explained that such information helped components fulfill their bill-paying and audit responsibilities. On the other hand, based on our review of customer bills for other shared services and information gathered during our focus groups, we found that other shared service accounts do not always provide enough information for customers to understand the basis for actual charges or fulfill bill-paying and audit responsibilities.

Our review of billing statements from various shared service accounts revealed various levels of detail on billing statements. Some bills had detailed information specifying the basis of every charge; however, one bill included an account service fee of over $20,000 without any explanation. Similarly, during our focus groups, finance staff responsible for paying for the shared services provided noted that billing adjustments sometimes appear without any explanation. Further, they said that JMD does not always provide complete billing information in a timely manner, especially in cases where customers are billed for a different amount than they had expected to pay at the beginning of the year. This inhibits customers' ability to anticipate their actual charges at the end of the year and undermines their ability to properly account for these costs. Customers also said that the follow-up necessary to obtain more information on these charges is time consuming and resource intensive.

Some customers do not receive complete, timely billing information because customers do not always provide JMD with contact information for individuals with responsibility for paying bills. Working capital fund account managers told us that they primarily communicate information such as rates, projected charges, and periodic reports to the points of contact listed in the interagency agreements. Customers can identify up to two customer points of contact in these agreements. However, JMD officials noted that while customers sometimes include program staff as the points of contact, finance staff contacts are not always identified.

JMD officials said that they expect the designated points of contact to pass information along to the right people within the components, as appropriate. JMD budget officials acknowledged that communication challenges exist within the components and that the information may not be getting to the appropriate staff. However, they also noted that it is the customer's responsibility to communicate billing information internally with its finance staff. While this is not an unreasonable expectation, we believe that helping to ensure that the right information gets to the right people at the right time is part of providing good customer service.

JMD Does Not Measure Customer Satisfaction with or the Cost-effectiveness of Its Shared Services

JMD Does Not Systematically Assess Customer Satisfaction with Its Shared Services

JMD does not systematically assess customer satisfaction with its services. A JMD official explained that this is the case because officials rely on JMD staff directors to gather customer feedback at a frequency appropriate for their specific services. A working capital fund staff director we spoke with said that JMD solicited customer input on an informal basis and had conducted surveys at the customers' request. The surveys we reviewed requested customer feedback on measures such as satisfaction and timeliness of services provided as well as whether improvements are needed. Absent a formal mechanism for customers to provide regular, timely feedback about working capital fund services, JMD cannot sufficiently assess whether customer needs are being met or have changed. As we have previously reported, establishing performance measures and goals for shared services is a critical management tool that can help an agency understand whether each of the working capital fund services it provides meet customer needs.[13]

JMD Does Not Measure the Cost-effectiveness of Its Shared Services

JMD has not assessed its shared services to know whether they provide a good value to customers, and therefore has not shared information about the cost-effectiveness of its services with customers. In our focus groups, customers said that although they expect the shared services to

---

[13] GAO-12-56.

offer them economies of scale—and customers assume that they are in fact getting a good value—JMD has not provided data that demonstrate this. Customers explained that having this information is especially important in light of the tight fiscal conditions they expect to face in the foreseeable future. In fact, one customer noted that his staff will be evaluating whether shared services purchased by his component are cost effective.

Providing information about the cost-effectiveness of shared services would also help JMD provide better customer service, in keeping with the President's efforts to streamline and improve service delivery.[14] Further, without conducting analysis to ensure that working capital fund services are a good value, JMD cannot use performance information to improve its own operations.[15] Lastly, data on the cost-effectiveness of shared services can help JMD customers meet the determination requirement of the Economy Act. When ordering services under the Economy Act, customers—as ordering agencies—must determine that the order is in the best interest of the government and cannot be procured as conveniently or inexpensively by contracting directly with the private sector.[16] Although JMD, as the performing agency, is not required to provide information to customers to help them make this determination, it has a business interest in helping other Justice components, which are the bulk of the working capital fund's customers, comply with these requirements.

JMD Does Not Assess Whether the Working Capital Fund Is Effectively Managed

Performance measures that are aligned with strategic, departmentwide goals can facilitate assessments on whether working capital fund activities are contributing to agency goals. JMD tracks and monitors the performance of its shared services provision on a limited, ad hoc basis. For example, JMD tracks workload measures, such as the number of

---

[14] Exec. Order No. 13,571, *Streamlining Service Delivery and Improving Customer Service,* 76 Fed. Reg. 24,339 (May 2, 2011).

[15] GAO-12-56.

[16] 31 U.S.C. § 1535. In addition, the Federal Acquisition Regulation requires that each Economy Act order be supported by a determination and finding stating that the interagency acquisition is in the best interest of the government and that the supplies or services cannot be as conveniently or economically procured by contracting directly with a private source. 48 C.F.R. 17.503(a).

personnel actions completed, number of transactions processed, and computer processing unit hours available. However, JMD does not have measures to assess how effectively it manages the fund, such as whether managers are responsive to customer issues on rates or billing—two areas with which customers have expressed concern.

A fiscal year 1997 financial audit of the fund tasked account managers with outlining major objectives and developing performance measures for the working capital fund. However, JMD officials told us that this had not been accomplished for all the department's shared services accounts before fiscal year 2007, when Justice rolled the financial, performance, and accountability audits of the working capital fund into Justice's audit of the Offices, Boards, and Divisions (OBD).[17] Accordingly, JMD officials told us that the working capital fund no longer receives its own audited financial statements; instead Justice develops performance measures for the OBD, under which the working capital fund audits were consolidated. This audit approach does not provide JMD with an opportunity to specifically measure working capital fund-level performance. In its agency comments, Justice clarified that while the working capital fund is part of a broader audited financial statement, performance measures are continually tracked and maintained through the department's Quarterly Status Report process during budget execution activities. Nevertheless, as we noted earlier, the workload measures that are tracked do not assess whether the fund is effectively managed, which is a key operating principle for working capital funds.

Since the fund's creation in 1975, changes in the work environment, technologies, budget conditions, agency needs, and long-term efficiencies have had an impact on how JMD provides shared services to its customers. Therefore, opportunities exist for JMD to evaluate whether the working capital fund provides shared services efficiently or the services are aligned with current departmental needs. For example, customers told us that while they need most services provided by the working capital fund, JMD has required them to use some services despite customers' ability to provide these services themselves. Specifically, one customer said that although her component had

---

[17] Justice's OBD comprises legal, executive, and management organizations. The working capital fund's financial statements are prepared as part of OBD's consolidated statement. Although financial audits occur at the OBD level, management and oversight of the fund remains a responsibility of JMD.

received appropriations to develop security training, it was required to purchase the same training from the working capital fund a few years later. She questioned whether components could have provided this training more cheaply and effectively than JMD. Another customer said that although his component owned and preferred its own audio equipment, it was required to use speakers and microphones provided by the working capital fund whenever events were held in the main Justice building. Both customers stated that JMD should assess whether the working capital fund should continue to provide those services for all components.

If available, specific working capital fund-level performance information would allow JMD to regularly compare actual performance with planned or expected performance. Making adjustments to the fund management and services, as appropriate, in a corresponding management review process could help JMD achieve the efficiencies that working capital funds were designed to produce, potentially freeing up resources that could be realigned for other departmental initiatives. Further, such a review could also allow JMD to better reassess functions to ensure that the working capital fund continues to provide the critical underlying infrastructure and support that allow other Justice components to perform their primary functions. Performance measures that are aligned with strategic goals can be used to evaluate whether and, if so, how working capital fund activities are contributing to the achievement of agency goals and departmentwide crosscutting initiatives.

Justice's Excess Unobligated Balances Have Been Unavailable for Departmental Priorities in Recent Years

Justice has the authority to capture excess unobligated balances into the working capital fund and AFF to fund various departmental priorities. These balances are available until expended. Specifically, the AFF balance—known as the Super Surplus—may be used for any authorized law enforcement purpose, while the working capital fund's Unobligated Balance Transfers account—known as UBT—may be used for capital investments or administrative purposes.

According to the AAG/A, who has responsibility for managing these authorities as Justice's Chief Financial Officer, the working capital fund and AFF's authority to retain and use transferred excess unobligated balances is a tremendous benefit for the department. He considers these authorities to be part of a suite of financial tools available to manage projects to meet Justice priorities.

Excess unobligated balances from accounts across the department can be transferred into the working capital fund's UBT. This account consists of moneys from expired Justice appropriation balances that are not needed to cover obligations or other adjustments and are about to be canceled.[18] Excess unobligated balances in AFF can be transferred into the Super Surplus account.[19] The Super Surplus amounts include prior-year declared excess unobligated balances. The Assets Forfeiture Management Staff, in conjunction with JMD budget staff, determine the amounts needed to (1) maintain AFF solvency by covering anticipated forfeiture-related expenses, (2) ensure a reserve for pending equitable forfeited assets and third-party payments with partners and victims (referred to as major sharing reserves), and (3) retain funding to cover rescissions. Any remaining funds can be declared as excess unobligated balances and used to increase the Super Surplus balance.

Justice leadership uses a four-step process to make final decisions on how to use the working capital fund's UBT and AFF's Super Surplus.

1. When excess unobligated balances are available, Justice components submit requests for funds to JMD. These requests must provide sufficient justification to allow senior Justice officials to make informed decisions about the use of these funds.
2. JMD budget staff consider each funding request in light of the priority resource needs of the department and the authorized purposes for which UBT and Super Surplus balances are available. JMD budget staff present their recommendations to the AAG/A for review and approval.

---

[18] Appropriations available for a definite period are canceled 5 fiscal years after the period of availability for obligations ends. Once balances are canceled, the amounts are unavailable for any purpose.

[19] The Comprehensive Crime Control Act of 1984 established AFF. AFF receives proceeds of forfeitures and pays for the costs associated with such forfeitures, including the costs of managing and disposing property; satisfying valid liens, mortgages, and other innocent owner claims; and other costs associated with accomplishing the legal forfeiture of property. The Attorney General is authorized to use AFF to pay any necessary expenses associated with forfeiture operations, such as property seizures, detention, management, forfeiture, and disposal. In responding to agency comments, Justice officials said that the AFF also has limited authority to finance certain general investigative expenses.

3. The AAG/A, with input from the Attorney General and other departmental leaders, makes the final decision on how to allocate these balances.
4. Before using the excess unobligated balances, JMD notifies OMB and the House and Senate Appropriations Committees' Commerce, Justice, and Science Subcommittees on how much they will use from the UBT and Super Surplus and for what purpose. While Justice is only required to notify Congress and OMB of its uses, it generally waits for approval before using the funds.

In the past, Justice has used the working capital fund UBT to fund general administrative acquisitions, such as improving Justice's financial management system. However, JMD budget officials told us that the UBT has not been available for departmental priorities in recent years. Since fiscal year 1995, Justice has used the UBT for rescissions enacted in law and drawn from the working capital fund. When rescinded amounts were equal to or greater than the existing UBT balance, those funds were unavailable for departmental priorities (see table 2).

Table 2: Working Capital Fund Unobligated Balance Transfers and Rescissions

Dollars in millions

	FY 2008	FY 2009	FY 2010	FY 2011
UBT deposits	$181	$90	$75	$114
Working capital fund rescission	41	100	0	26
UBT available for agency priorities	140	0	75	88

Sources: Justice documents, GAO analysis of the President's Budget Appendixes for the working capital fund as well as fiscal year 2011 appropriations acts, and JMD officials.

When AFF Super Surplus balances were available, Justice allocated funding for various law enforcement purposes as determined by the Attorney General's statutory discretion, such as programs targeting crimes against children. Because rescissions from AFF have been greater than the existing Super Surplus balance since fiscal year 2008, the Super Surplus has been unavailable for departmental priorities in recent years. Further, an amount equal to the prior fiscal year's rescission has been designated for return to the AFF Super Surplus the following fiscal year (see table 3).[20]

Table 3: Super Surplus Balances and AFF Rescissions

Dollars in millions

	FY 2008	FY 2009	FY 2010	FY 2011
Super Surplus balance	$55	$45	$207	$79
AFF rescission	240	285	387	495

Source: GAO analysis of Assets Forfeiture Management Staff documents and the President's Budget Appendixes for the Assets Forfeiture Fund.

Conclusions

Working capital funds provide agencies with an opportunity to operate more efficiently by consolidating and providing services. They also create incentives for customers and managers to exercise cost control and economic restraint. Given the fiscal pressures facing the federal government, consolidating operations could potentially achieve cost savings and help agencies provide more efficient and effective services. Agencies can maximize the potential of these opportunities by following four key working capital fund operating principles. Specifically, these principles are to clearly delineate roles and responsibilities, ensure self-sufficiency by recovering the agency's actual costs, measure performance, and build in flexibility to obtain customer input and meet customer needs. JMD effectively tracks working capital fund moneys in accordance with fiscal law, clearly delineates roles and responsibilities within the fund, and ensures self-sufficiency by recovering total shared services costs. Further, customers noted positive benefits from shared services, including the breadth of services offered, the experience and knowledge of shared services staff, and the convenience and ease of having these services provided in-house.

[20] The President's Budget designates a return of Super Surplus each fiscal year in an amount equal to the prior fiscal year's rescission. However, AFF's appropriation for that fiscal year does not specifically provide for such a return of the Super Surplus. In responding to a draft of this report, Assets Forfeiture Management Staff told us that AFF rescissions to date are temporary in that the rescinded amounts are not transferred out of the AFF at any time, but are unavailable for obligation during the fiscal year of the rescission. When the fiscal year in which the rescission occurred expires, the AFF moneys are then available for use in the following fiscal years unless and until another rescission is enacted.

Customers do not always understand the basis for the rates they pay and lack assurances that fund costs are equitably distributed among customers. Although JMD established the CAB to improve customer satisfaction with the working capital fund, board members do not find the annual meeting—JMD's primary vehicle for engaging board members about shared services and their accompanying rates—a useful forum in which to understand and provide advice on fund management and operations. Further, JMD does not have a systematic way to communicate with non-CAB customers, which results in uneven flow and availability of information among working capital fund customers, especially regarding the structures of some shared services rates. JMD officials described various ways that they push information on rates and services out to their customers but ultimately agreed that some customers may have better access to this information than others, and said that they remained committed to continuing to improve communication with customers. Providing ample opportunity for customers to provide input on services and voice their concerns about the fund is a key principle for managing working capital funds. Further, transparent and equitable pricing methodologies allow agencies to ensure that shared services rates charged recover agencies' actual costs and reflect customers' service usage. If customers understand how rates are determined, they can better anticipate changes to assumptions, identify their effect on costs, and incorporate this information into their budget planning.

Customer experiences with getting clear, timely, well-explained bills for working capital fund services are mixed, and our review of customer bills for shared services found that some services do not always provide enough information for the customers to understand the basis for the charges contained in the bills. As a result, customers' ability to anticipate their actual charges at the end of the year and to properly account for these costs was inhibited. Although customers do not always provide JMD with points of contact for billing information, we believe that helping to ensure that the right information gets to the right people at the right time is part of providing good customer service.

Although JMD tracks and monitors limited performance information for some shared services, it does not have measures to assess how effectively it manages the fund, such as whether managers are responsive to customer inquiries or billing error rates—two areas with which customers have expressed concern. By establishing performance measures and goals for working capital fund operations that align with Justice's strategic goals, and putting a management review process in place to track fund performance, JMD would have the necessary tools to know whether the fund is achieving the efficiencies that intragovernmental revolving funds were designed to produce. Absent a systematic way to measure customer satisfaction with shared services as well as fund-level performance, JMD is missing an opportunity to identify potential improvements and efficiencies to the services it provides. Further, by better understanding the fund's effectiveness, JMD could potentially free up resources that could be realigned for other departmental priorities.

Recommendations for Executive Action

To improve the management of the Justice working capital fund, we recommend that the Attorney General direct the AAG/A to take the following three actions:

1. Improve opportunities for two-way substantive communication with shared services customers. This could include developing a means to discuss customer concerns about working capital fund rates and services; organizing breakout sessions on specific lines of business, to be attended by appropriate customer program and finance staff; restructuring the annual CAB meetings to allow further opportunities for two-way communication; conducting a periodic survey or listening session with customers on such topics as their level of satisfaction or potential changes to service needs; or a combination of these.

2. Help ensure that information on the basis of rates for each shared services and sufficiently detailed billing information reaches the appropriate customer staff, especially those in the finance and program offices. This could include posting relevant portions of the operating plan with information on the basis of rate structures on Justice's intranet, requiring both a program office and finance point of contact to be provided in each reimbursable agreement, or organizing periodic dedicated sessions for both program staff and finance customer staff to discuss issues relevant to them.

3. Develop performance measures to monitor whether all shared services are provided in an efficient and effective manner. These measures should support goals that align with Justice priorities and, as the departmental needs change over time, provide JMD additional assurance that the level and types of working capital fund services provided support current departmental goals.

Agency Comments and Our Evaluation

We provided a draft of this report to the Attorney General for official review and comment. In his letter, which is reprinted in appendix III, the Assistant Attorney General for Administration generally agreed with our findings and recommendations. Specifically, he noted that JMD will continue to explore ways to address the issues we identified. For the third recommendation, he noted that while it is possible to enhance oversight of the working capital fund by formulating and tracking additional performance measures, such measures would not be necessary to assure Justice that fund services support the department's needs. While we agree that fund services provide critical support to Justice's mission, we continue to believe that as the departmental needs change over time, JMD could provide additional assurance that the level and types of working capital fund services provided support current agency goals. Further, we have revised the third recommendation to reflect this. Justice provided technical comments, which we incorporated as appropriate.

We are sending copies of this report to the Attorney General and other interested parties. In addition, the report is available at no charge on the GAO website at http://www.gao.gov.

If you or your staff have any questions about this report, please contact me at (202) 512-6806 or fantoned@gao.gov. Contact points for our Offices of Congressional Relations and Public Affairs may be found on the last page of this report. Major contributors to this report are listed in appendix IV.

Denise M. Fantone
Director, Strategic Issues

Appendix I: Other Working Capital Fund Services and Customers

The following tables show the interactive data from figure 1. Table 4 shows working capital fund amounts for services and support for "other services." Table 5 shows working capital fund amounts for customers under "all other customers."

Table 4: Working Capital Fund Services and Support – "Other Services"

Services and support	Dollar amount
Financial management services	$29 million
Human resource systems	$28 million
Enterprise solutions staff	$13 million
Library acquisitions service	$12 million
Human resources	$11 million
E-government services staff	$8 million
Assets forfeiture management staff	$3 million
Program review services	$3 million

Source: Justice documents.

Table 5: Working Capital Fund Customers – "All Other Customers"

All other customers	Dollar amount
U.S. Trustee Program	$44 million
General Administration	$43 million
Justice Information Sharing Technology	$41 million
Criminal Division	$41 million
Executive Office for Immigration Review	$40 million
Department of Homeland Security	$38 million
Antitrust Division	$31 million
U.S. Marshals Service	$28 million
Bureau of Alcohol, Tobacco, Firearms and Explosives	$26 million
Civil Rights Division	$22 million
Office of Justice Programs	$21 million
Environment and Natural Resources Division	$20 million
National Security Division	$17 million
Tax Division	$17 million
Other users	$14 million
Community Oriented Policing Services	$13 million
Office of the Inspector General	$12 million

All other customers	Dollar amount
Assets Forfeiture	$9 million
Narrowband Communications	$8 million
Federal Prison Industries	$6 million
National Drug Intelligence Center	$5 million
Interpol	$4 million
Office on Violence Against Women	$4 million
Fees and Expenses of Witnesses	$3 million
Community Relations Service	$2 million
Office of Legal Counsel	$2 million
Solicitor General	$2 million
United States Parole Commission	$1 million
International Criminal Investigative Training Assistance Program	$1 million
Court Services and Offender Supervision Agency	$1 million
Office of the Federal Detention Trustee	$1 million

Source: Justice documents.

Appendix II: Key Operating Principles for Managing Working Capital Funds

Principle	Components of principle	Examples of evidence supporting principle
Clearly delineate roles and responsibilities Appropriate delineation of roles and responsibilities promotes a clear understanding of who will be held accountable for specific tasks or duties, such as authorizing and reviewing transactions, implementing controls over working capital fund management, and helping to ensure that related responsibilities are coordinated. In addition, this reduces the risk of mismanaged funds and tasks or functions "falling through the cracks." Moreover, it helps customers know who to contact if they have questions.	Segregate duties to reduce error or fraud	Written roles and responsibilities specify how key duties and respons bilities are divided across multiple individuals/offices and are subject to a process of checks and balances. This should include separating responsibilities for authorizing transactions, processing and recording them, and reviewing the transactions.
	Define key areas of authority and responsibility	Written description of all working capital fund roles and responsibilities is available in an accessible format, such as a fund manual. Discussions with providers and clients confirm a clear understanding.
	Establish management review and approval process at the functional or activity level that ensures appropriate tracking and use of funds	A routine review process exists to ensure proper execution of transactions and events.
Ensure self-sufficiency by recovering the agency's actual costs Transparent and equitable pricing methodologies allow agencies to ensure that rates charged recover agencies' actual costs and reflect customers' service usage. If customers understand how rates are determined or changed, including the assumptions used, customers can better anticipate potential changes to those assumptions, identify their effect on costs, and incorporate that information into budget plans. A management review process can help to ensure that the methodology is applied consistently over time and provides a forum to inform customers of decisions and discuss as needed.	Establish transparent and equitable pricing methodology	Published price sheets for services are readily available. Documentation of pricing formulas supports equitable distribution of costs.
	Set rates to cover agency's total costs of providing service	Pricing methodology and accompanying process ensure that in aggregate, charges recover the actual costs of operations.
	Establish management review for rate setting	Management review process allows fund managers to receive and incorporate feedback from customers. Discussions with customers confirm an understanding of the charges and that they are viewed as transparent and equitable.
Measure performance Performance goals and measures are important management tools applicable to all operations of an agency, including the program, project, or activity levels. Performance measures and goals could include targets that assess fund managers' responsiveness to customer inquiries, the consistency in the application of the funds' rate-setting methodology, and the billing error rates. Performance measures that are aligned with strategic goals can be used to evaluate whether and, if so, how working capital fund activities are contributing to the achievement of agency goals. A	Establish performance measures and goals	Performance indicators and metrics for working capital fund management (not just for the services provided) are documented.
	Align performance measures with strategic goals	Indicators or metrics to measure outputs and outcomes are aligned with strategic goals and working capital fund priorities.

Principle	Components of principle	Examples of evidence supporting principle
management review process comparing expected to actual performance allows agencies to review progress toward goals and potentially identify ways to improve performance.	Establish management review of working capital fund performance	Working capital fund managers regularly compare actual performance with planned or expected results and make improvements as appropriate. In addition, performance results are periodically benchmarked against standards or "best in class" in a specific activity.
Build in flexibility to obtain customer input and meet customer needs Opportunities for customers to provide input about working capital fund services, or voice concerns about needs, in a timely manner enable agencies to regularly assess whether customer needs are being met or have changed. This also enables agencies to prioritize customer demands and use resources most effectively, enabling them to adjust working capital fund capacity up or down as business rises or falls.	Communicate with customers regularly and in a timely manner	An established forum, routine meetings, surveys, or a combination of these solicit information on customer needs and satisfaction with working capital fund performance.
	Develop process to assess resources needed to meet changes in customer demand	Established communication channels regularly and actively seek information on changes in customer demand and assess the resources needed to accommodate those changes.
	Establish process to prioritize requests for services	Established management review process allows for trade-off decisions to prioritize and shift limited resources needed to accommodate changes in demand across the organization.

Source: GAO analysis.

Appendix III: Comments from the Department of Justice

U.S. Department of Justice

Washington, D.C. 20530

JAN 13 2012

Ms. Denise M. Fontane
Director, Strategic Issues
U.S. Government Accountability Office
441 G Street, NW
Washington, DC 20548

Dear Ms. Fontane:

The Department of Justice has reviewed the Government Accountability Office's (GAO) draft report "Working Capital Fund Adheres to Some Key Operating Principles But Could Better Measure Performance and Communicate with Customers (GAO-12-289)."

The Department agrees with GAO's findings on how the Justice Management Division (JMD) 1) effectively tracks Working Capital Fund (WCF) functions to ensure adherence to applicable fiscal laws and sound management practices, 2) has well-established policies and procedures for tracking and monitoring the four WCF functions, 3) clearly delineates roles and responsibilities, and 4) has processes in place to ensure that excess unobligated balances are used in accordance with legal authorities.

The GAO made three recommendations in its draft report.

GAO RECOMMENDATION # 1: Improve opportunities for two-way substantive communication with shared services customers. This could include developing a means to discuss customer concerns about working capital fund rates and services; organizing breakout sessions on specific lines of business, to be attended by appropriate customer program and finance staff; restructuring the annual customer advisory board meetings to allow further opportunities for two-way communication; and/or conducting a periodic survey or listening session with customers on such topics as their level of satisfaction or potential changes to service needs.

DOJ RESPONSE: The Department agrees that communication between the WCF and customers is important and has taken many steps to improve it over the years, including establishing the Customer Advisory Board (CAB), holding annual CAB meetings, issuing memoranda on WCF operations, and posting customer-oriented information on the Department's internet and intranet websites. The Department will continue to explore ways to make CAB meetings more beneficial and to provide other mechanisms for soliciting customer feedback.

2

GAO RECOMMENDATION # 2: Help ensure that information on the basis of rates for each shared service and detailed billing information reaches the appropriate customer staff, especially those in the finance and program offices. This could include posting relevant portions of the operating plan with information on the basis of rate structures on Justice's intranet, requiring both a program office and finance point of contact in each reimbursable agreement, or organizing periodic dedicated sessions for both program staff and finance customer staff to discuss issues relevant to them.

DOJ RESPONSE: The Department agrees that communication plays an integral role in ensuring that important information reaches the right people. The Department agrees that this can be improved and will consider posting additional WCF-related information on the internet and intranet websites. As noted in the report, the Department already posts important WCF rate information on the internet and intranet websites.

GAO RECOMMENDATION # 3: Develop performance measures to monitor whether all shared services are provided in an efficient and effective manner. These measures should support goals that align with Justice priorities and assure JMD that the levels and types of working capital fund services provided support current departmental needs.

DOJ RESPONSE: As noted in the report, the WCF already utilizes performance and workload measures. It is possible to enhance oversight of the WCF by formulating and tracking additional performance measures to ensure they align with the Department's strategic goals. However, such measures would not be necessary to reassure the Department that WCF services support the Department's needs. All WCF services are considered critical and essential to promoting the Department's mission. These services include those based on laws, Executive Branch directives and priorities determined by the Attorney General.

The Department appreciates this opportunity to comment on the draft report prepared by the GAO.

Should you have any questions regarding this topic, please do not hesitate to contact Richard Theis, DOJ Audit Liaison at 202-514-0469.

Sincerely,

Lee J. Lofthus
Assistant Attorney General
   for Administration

Appendix IV: GAO Contact and Staff Acknowledgments

GAO Contact	Denise M. Fantone, (202) 512-6806 or fantoned@gao.gov
Staff Acknowledgments	In addition to the contact named above, Jacqueline M. Nowicki, Assistant Director, and Shirley Hwang, Analyst-in-Charge, managed this assignment. Melissa L. King, Catherine H. Myrick, and Keith C. O'Brien made major contributions to this report. Cynthia Saunders provided methodological assistance, Felicia Lopez provided legal assistance, and Donna Miller developed the report's graphics. Other individuals providing key advice included Sandra Burrell, Samantha Carter, and Jack Warner.

GAO's Mission	The Government Accountability Office, the audit, evaluation, and investigative arm of Congress, exists to support Congress in meeting its constitutional responsibilities and to help improve the performance and accountability of the federal government for the American people. GAO examines the use of public funds; evaluates federal programs and policies; and provides analyses, recommendations, and other assistance to help Congress make informed oversight, policy, and funding decisions. GAO's commitment to good government is reflected in its core values of accountability, integrity, and reliability.
Obtaining Copies of GAO Reports and Testimony	The fastest and easiest way to obtain copies of GAO documents at no cost is through GAO's website (www.gao.gov). Each weekday afternoon, GAO posts on its website newly released reports, testimony, and correspondence. To have GAO e-mail you a list of newly posted products, go to www.gao.gov and select "E-mail Updates."
Order by Phone	The price of each GAO publication reflects GAO's actual cost of production and distribution and depends on the number of pages in the publication and whether the publication is printed in color or black and white. Pricing and ordering information is posted on GAO's website, http://www.gao.gov/ordering.htm. Place orders by calling (202) 512-6000, toll free (866) 801-7077, or TDD (202) 512-2537. Orders may be paid for using American Express, Discover Card, MasterCard, Visa, check, or money order. Call for additional information.
Connect with GAO	Connect with GAO on Facebook, Flickr, Twitter, and YouTube. Subscribe to our RSS Feeds or E-mail Updates. Listen to our Podcasts. Visit GAO on the web at www.gao.gov.
To Report Fraud, Waste, and Abuse in Federal Programs	Contact: Website: www.gao.gov/fraudnet/fraudnet.htm E-mail: fraudnet@gao.gov Automated answering system: (800) 424-5454 or (202) 512-7470
Congressional Relations	Ralph Dawn, Managing Director, dawnr@gao.gov, (202) 512-4400 U.S. Government Accountability Office, 441 G Street NW, Room 7125 Washington, DC 20548
Public Affairs	Chuck Young, Managing Director, youngc1@gao.gov, (202) 512-4800 U.S. Government Accountability Office, 441 G Street NW, Room 7149 Washington, DC 20548